ABOUT THIS BOOK

Our book tells the story of the life of one particular elephant over a single year. We have written and illustrated our story as if we had watched the elephant's behavior through the year, noticing how its activities changed at different periods. By looking closely at one elephant, we give you a good understanding of how an individual animal reacts to others and to the conditions it experiences in the wild.

We have called our elephant Mbili. On pages 4 and 5 we show you where Mbili lives and tell you a little about ⬚⬚⬚⬚ Our main story, on ⬚⬚⬚⬚ in Mbili's life, and i⬚⬚⬚⬚ between one and ⬚⬚⬚ ⬚⬚ long. Each section begins with a large illustration showing the environment and one aspect of Mbili's behavior at that time. The following two pages in each section continue our main story and show some of Mbili's other activities during the same period. We have followed our main story with a section on elephant conservation.

INTRODUCTION

In the past two million years many kinds of elephant have lived. Now only two kinds remain, the Asian and the African.

Elephants are the largest living land animals. They eat only plants, in very large quantities. They have 24 huge grinding teeth, 12 on each side of their jaw. These grow in turn from the back of the jaw so that not more than eight are in use at the same time. When the last teeth are worn down the elephant can no longer chew, and starves. But an elephant has a lifespan of about 60 years.

The most distinctive features of an elephant are its tusks and its trunk. The tusks, made of ivory, are a pair of elongated upper incisor teeth. They can grow 10 feet long. The trunk is a long nose and upper lip, and contains thousands of muscles. It is strong but also can be used delicately. It helps the elephant breathe, smell, feed, drink, scratch, explore, caress, and make noises.

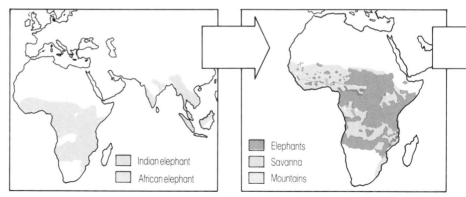

△ The map shows the distribution of both living species of elephant. The African elephant, scientific name *Loxodonta africana*, is still found over much of Africa south of the Sahara.

△ Elephants live in both forested and open grassland, or savanna, areas. Savanna elephants, such as those from East Africa described in this book, are generally the larger of the two.

Mbili – an African elephant

The male elephants, called bulls, grow to a height of 12 feet at the shoulder and can weigh about 7 tons. Females, cows, rarely grow more than 9 feet tall and about 4 tons in weight. Our elephant, Mbili, is a young cow elephant. Baby elephants are called calves.

Elephants have good senses of smell and hearing but their eyesight is not as good as ours. They live in herds consisting of closely related elephants.

The environment

In East Africa, Mbili's home, there is no distinct spring, summer, autumn, or winter. It is warm or hot almost all year round. But it can be cooler high up in the mountains, especially at night. The nights are always about 12 hours long. Yet there are some changes in a year. Generally there are two periods when rain falls, each lasting several weeks. In between the rainy periods it is very dry. Our story begins during a dry period.

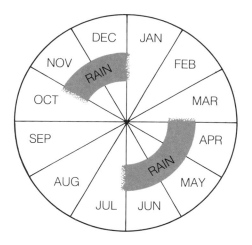

The calendar in Mbili's home area. A small calendar is used in the main story to show the time span of each section.

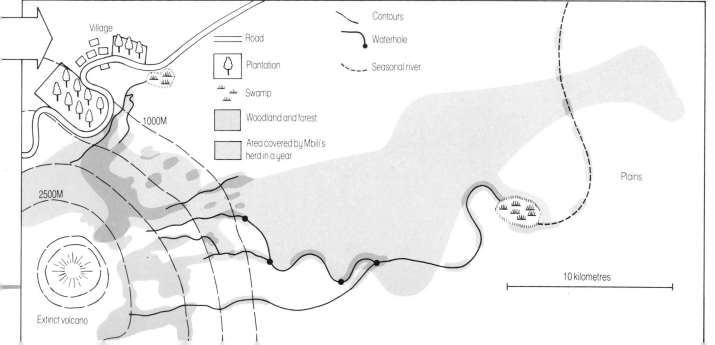

5

Mbili moved with the herd across the wide plain. For months there had been no rain and the ground was parched, the grass dry and yellow. Even the scattered trees looked dry and withered. The elephants tore up tufts of grass with the tips of their trunks, then banged off the loose earth and gobbled up and chewed the tufts as they moved on. Even this tough dry food would satisfy their hunger, but they were short of water. They kept on the move towards an

6

area they had visited before where a small river ran across the grassland.

Mbili's mother led the way most of the time. She was thirty-four years old, the oldest and most experienced elephant in the herd. Mbili was only twelve years old, just about adult but not fully grown. She was the fourth oldest in the herd, after her mother, aunt, and elder sister.

The elephants did not seem to be hurrying but they had already walked many miles that day.

They had started before the sun was up. Mbili stopped for a moment at a baobab tree and gashed its bark with her tusks. But the tree was empty. Another herd had already raided it for the water stored in its trunk.

Just before midday the elephants came within sight of the river. But when they arrived at the watercourse, they found the river dried up. No water was to be seen. They retreated into the shade of trees, fanning their ears to keep cool.

Water at last

As the day became cooler the elephants renewed their search for water. Mbili walked to the river bed and sniffed the earth. She scuffed up some sand with one of her front feet. She sniffed again, then she dug more quickly using her tusks and trunk. Soon she had made a large hole. Water seeped into the bottom and Mbili waited to gather a trunkful. By now all the adults were digging. The young gathered round. Before nightfall all the herd had drunk their fill.

△▷ Elephants can dig down to water that other animals cannot reach. They suck water up into their trunks, as much as 4 quarts at a time, then squirt it down their throats. They also dig for salt, which helps balance their diet, especially in the dry season.

8

Testing the air

As the sun came up the next day a gentle breeze blew briefly across the plain. Mbili raised her trunk and tested the air. She used her sensitive nose to investigate her surroundings. She could smell damp green plants away in the distance. Soon after the sun had begun to bake the ground again, the breeze vanished, but Mbili's mother had noticed the scent too and for the whole day led the herd in the direction from which the smell had come.

Keeping cool

The herd kept going for several hours after nightfall before resting. The next day the elephants reached and climbed some hills. Here they found a few streams from which they could drink, and the grasses and trees were not so dried up as those on the plain.

Most of the time the elephants kept on the move, but during the heat of the day they sheltered in the shade of tall thorn trees.

▷ An elephant's ears have many blood vessels and act as radiators to give off unwanted heat from its body. The hotter the weather, the harder it flaps its ears.

THE RAINS BEGIN

For two weeks Mbili and her family wandered in the hills. They felt more comfortable here. There was more shelter from the sun and it was a little cooler than the plain. The food was better too. One day Mbili's mother led the herd above the hills and onto the slopes of the mountain that stretched above. Here was thick forest bathed in cloud. Mbili walked silently through the forest. The trees towered above her. There were few leaves and fruits within easy reach, so she felt happier when they emerged into the sun again and she found some juicy grass.

Out in the open, Mbili sensed a change. Clouds were appearing in the sky over the plain, first white, then dark and threatening. A wind stirred. Then came a far-off crackle of thunder. The elephants milled about, not frightened but excited. Suddenly a hissing drumming sound came toward them and the rains began. First a few drops appeared, then pelting driving rain. Even such big animals felt the need to shelter, and Mbili and her family huddled close behind a rocky outcrop.

As the storm broke, the hill streams were suddenly changed into fast-flowing rivers and plants began to grow rapidly. It was the start of a good time for Mbili, with plenty of food and water. But there were dangers too. Mbili's little sister got stuck at the bottom of a muddy bank along one of the swollen streams. Mbili and her mother had to work hard together, pushing and pulling, to get her out. At last the little animal was able to scramble up the bank to safety.

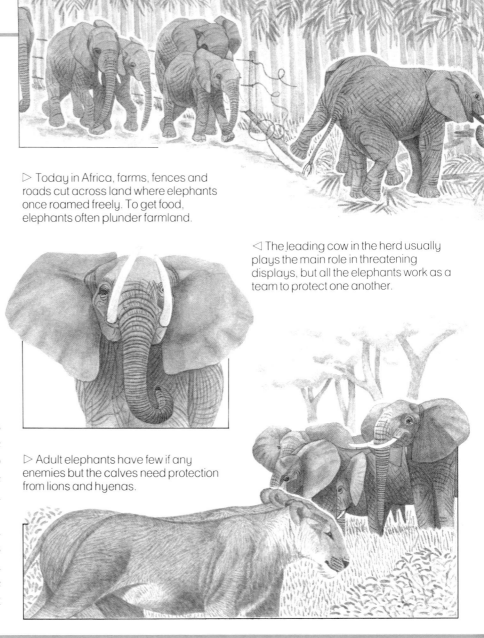

Freedom has limits

One day the elephants wandered farther than usual and at dusk came to a dirt road. Here was something new to them, a wire fence with strong posts. The elephants could smell ripe fruit beyond the fence. They pushed against the obstacle, and Mbili's mother uprooted one of the posts then flattened part of the fence. The elephants entered the banana plantation and fed. They stayed all night. At dawn the villagers saw them and came with rattles and anything else that would make a noise. The elephants fled.

Keeping on guard

On returning to familiar territory, they approached a waterhole. Mbili scented lion. The elephants drew close together, with the youngsters near the middle. Two lions were lying in wait in the bushes. Mbili's mother stepped forward with ears outstretched, suddenly tucked in her trunk and charged. The lions ran off. Mbili's mother stopped, snorted and shook her head, then went back to the herd. Now safe, the elephants went down to the waterhole.

▷ Today in Africa, farms, fences and roads cut across land where elephants once roamed freely. To get food, elephants often plunder farmland.

◁ The leading cow in the herd usually plays the main role in threatening displays, but all the elephants work as a team to protect one another.

▷ Adult elephants have few if any enemies but the calves need protection from lions and hyenas.

Frolics and fun

Mbili walked slowly into the water and for several minutes stood drinking. Then she sank down on her haunches and rolled onto her side, almost disappearing under the water. She splashed around waving her legs and using her trunk as a snorkel.

All the herd relaxed and played in the water. Mbili's young brother climbed on her and slid off into the water with an enormous splash. Even her tiny sister was squealing with delight as she ran up and down in the shallows.

Skin care

Eventually Mbili stood up and went to the bank, where she threw mud over her back. As the mud dried it formed a thick crust on her skin. Nearby she found some dry sand and blew it over her back and under her belly until it covered her. Then she moved to a termite mound and scratched her shoulder and rump against it contentedly.

▷ Elephants seem to enjoy all their skin care activities. When caked in mud, their skin may appear reddish or black rather than the normal gray.

△ ▽ An elephant's skin lacks sweat and grease glands so the animals must take care to keep their skin in good condition. Bathing helps keep the skin supple. Mud may help cool it and wards off insects that bite. Rubbing with sand and grit removes old dry skin.

FAMILIES MEET

It was late November. Green sprouts of grass were shooting up everywhere. Below the hills the ground looked lush and green again and gradually the elephants made their way down to the plains. Food was now plentiful. Mbili's family did not need to cover large distances each day to find enough leaves and grass. Sometimes they spread out over the bush country as they fed. Usually they could see and hear one another but there were days when Mbili's aunt and her two calves lost touch with the others and wandered by themselves. After a day or two they rejoined the herd.

There were other families of elephants on the plain. Most of these avoided Mbili and her family but a few were quite happy to mingle with them if the herds met. Mbili had met some of these elephants before and she greeted them as friends. She went toward one of them with her trunk stretched out until their trunk tips met. Then she put her trunk tip to the other elephant's head and into its mouth. They exchanged information by touch and scents. Sometimes two or three herds mingled together for several days but usually it was not long before Mbili's mother and the other herd leaders took their followers in different directions.

The elephants spent their days peacefully. As she fed, Mbili could hear around her the sounds made by other elephants as they cropped grass or tore twigs from bushes. She made a low contented rumbling growl which was answered by other members of the family.

The daily routine

Starting before dawn, Mbili and the other elephants alternately fed and moved a short distance. At midday they stopped and stood resting in shade. After an hour or two they became active again. In the evening the herd visited a waterhole to drink and bathe. After sunset it was cooler and this was when the elephants walked farthest. They slept only in the early hours of the morning, and then just for an hour or two.

△▷ Elephants sleep standing up or, unless they are particularly big and heavy, lying on one side. Lying down, they may rest their head on a pillow of vegetation. Elephants often snore in their sleep.

▽ Elephants feed in swamps as well as in savanna and forest. There the vegetation is often rather soft and easy to digest. Old elephants with worn teeth often make their home in swamps.

Feeding

Most of the time she was awake, Mbili was feeding. Each day she ate more than a person's weight in food. In the wet season the grass was sweet and this was her main food, but she also ate leaves, fruits, and twigs from bushes and trees. Later on in the year, when the grass was dry and withered, the taller plants formed the main part of her diet. Although she needed so much food, Mbili did not hurry her meals. She carefully selected each mouthful. With grass, Mbili curled the end of her trunk around a tuft and pulled, sometimes using her foot to help tear the blades.

△ A herd may spread out when feeding so that some animals disappear from sight among bushes. But the elephants keep in touch by the sounds that they make.

△ The average mouthful of leaves or grass an elephant eats weighs about as much as an apple. An adult may need 2,000 mouthfuls each day to satisfy its needs.

△ Elephant dung fertilizes the soil and is food to some beetles and other animals. Many seeds grow best if they have passed through an elephant's gut.

When feeding on bushes, she occasionally used the tips of her trunk like tweezers to pick a juicy morsel, but mostly she simply wrapped her trunk around a branch and stripped off all the leaves.

Once Mbili had put food in her mouth she ground it back and forth between her huge teeth and then swallowed. Much of the food was tough and difficult to digest. As it was fermenting in her gut, Mbili's stomach rumbled. While she was awake and feeding, she produced dung as often as once an hour. Some of the food was so tough it passed straight through her gut without being digested.

LIVING AS A HERD

The rains had stopped nearly as suddenly as they began. As the earth dried out, plant growth slowed and the grass started to brown. Mbili and the rest of the herd had no trouble finding food, but to get fresh leaves they had to stretch their trunks farther up into the trees. One day a herd of three bull elephants crossed their path. Being taller the bulls could stretch even higher for juicy titbits. And when they could not reach the branch they fancied, they used their great weight to break down the trees. Mbili was quick to make use of a thorn tree which a bull had toppled. The thorns did not stop her from eating the tasty young green upper leaves.

On this occasion the bulls did not take much notice of Mbili and her family. Mbili's mother was a little suspicious of the strangers but they seemed harmless and for three days the small herd of males and Mbili's herd fed in the same area. Then the males moved on, leaving more broken trees to mark their passage.

Mbili's herd traveled slowly, moving only a few miles each day. The youngest elephants had energy left to play and prodded and pushed one another. They sometimes tried this on the adults too and were gently pushed aside as the bigger animals went on feeding. Within the herd there were few arguments. After years together the elephants knew just how much they could tease one another.

19

A male approaches

A few days later the male elephants returned. These three were great wanderers. The eldest was a huge old bull who weighed over seven tons. The other bulls were each about 20 years old and weighed only around four tons – half as heavy again as Mbili.

Once again the bulls fed near the edge of Mbili's herd but this time there was trouble. One of the bulls came silently into a clearing where Mbili's family were feeding. He was reaching for a branch and did not notice two young elephants close by until he nearly walked into them. They suddenly saw the huge bull and trumpeted in alarm. Quickly Mbili's mother gave a squeal of rage and lumbered toward the intruder. Even though he was the larger, he backed away.

For several minutes the herd milled about in excitement. By the time they had calmed down the three bulls had moved far away. They did not come so close again.

▷ If a herd member is threatened, its companions rush to its aid. The leader may charge a supposed enemy. Bulls are usually gentle to females and calves.

Male group

Family group

◁ ▽ Most of the time, adult male elephants stay separate from the herds of females and young. Sometimes they travel in small bull groups but very old males live alone. Male elephants grow faster than females once they are of breeding age. Elephants seem to keep growing most of their lives.

Rivalry

Over the next three days Mbili saw the bulls several times. When they were not feeding, the two young bulls often wrestled. They stood head to head and pushed and pulled each other with their trunks. They did not use their tusks as weapons and just tested their strengths. One was somewhat stronger. Gradually he asserted his authority over the other. But neither tried to challenge the big bull. He was too strong for them.

An elephant's grave

As the herd reached a river, Mbili stumbled across an elephant skeleton. It had been picked clean of flesh by vultures and some of the bones had been gnawed by hyenas. Mbili smelled the bones, carefully turned a few over several times, then picked one up with the tip of her trunk. The bones puzzled her. They reminded her of elephant but she could not understand what they were. The other elephants were fascinated too, and as they moved off, some carried bones a little way before dropping them. It was like a parting gesture to an old friend.

▽ A dying elephant usually moves away from its herd to its final resting place. Elephants sometimes scatter the bones of dead elephants over a wide area.

A BIRTH IN THE HERD

For two months there had been no rain. Food and water were scarce. But now, in March, many elephants had their babies. In Mbili's herd, the only female that now had a baby was her elder sister. She had been pregnant for nearly twenty-two months but she did not look very fat. The only sign that a birth was due was a swelling of her two breasts which would provide milk for the newborn.

Early one morning Mbili's pregnant sister went and stood apart from the feeding herd. The birth began. After a few minutes Mbili and her mother moved to her sister's side. It was almost an hour before the baby emerged head-first and tumbled to the ground. It was still covered in a membrane. The mother nuzzled the baby with her trunk but was exhausted after the effort of the birth. Mbili helped her first to free the calf from the membrane then to nudge it to its feet for the first time using their trunks and forelegs. The baby staggered and fell back. At the third attempt it stood alone.

The new baby, a little cow elephant, stood almost three feet tall and her dark skin was covered with reddish-brown hair. For the first hours of her life the new baby alternately stood and fell over. Both mother and baby seemed hardly able to move. It was Mbili who stood over the baby protectively until her sister got her strength back. The herd did not travel far that day but by evening the baby was able to totter along between Mbili and her sister and the herd moved on.

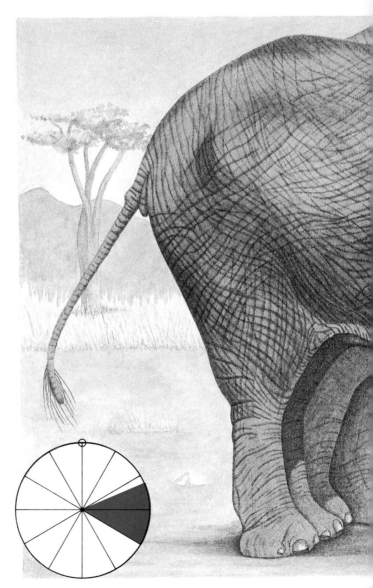

Caring for the young

The newborn baby soon began searching her mother's underside for food. At first she was not sure where to look but soon she found a teat and began suckling. She suckled with her mouth not her trunk. For her first year she would find her trunk of little use.

During the first few months of the baby's life, her mother rarely allowed her to stray more than a few feet away. The little elephant often leaned against and touched her mother, who in return caressed her with her trunk. At times Mbili took over from the mother and acted as a nursemaid.

△ Newborn elephants soon try to suckle but have to search for the teats between the mother's front legs. After a few months they eat some solids but they need milk until they are two years old.

◁ A calf will suck milk from other adult cows in the herd as well as from its mother and they do not seem to mind. Some calves suckle when too old to need milk, probably for comfort rather than food.

▷ Often a cow that is almost adult will act as an "aunt" to a calf. This helps the calf's mother and is good practice for when the cow has a calf of her own.

△ Cow elephants mate for the first time when about 11 years old. Bulls mature at a similar age but are rarely able to mate until they are older and big enough to drive off rival bulls.

△ Elephants sometimes spend time getting to know one another before they mate, but if the cow is ready, they mate soon after meeting. The female is in heat for only about two days at a time.

△ ▽ Love-play is often noisy but mating silent. A cow elephant mates and produces a single baby about once every four years. The male plays no part in looking after mother and baby.

Mating

Soon after the baby was born the rains came again, drenching the ground and starting a new burst of plant growth. It was at this time that Mbili first became ready to mate. The herd of three males was not far away. When the largest male scented that Mbili was "in heat," he drove off the other bulls and came looking for her.

Mbili was grazing when the male approached. She was uncertain of him but stood her ground and put out her trunk in greeting. The two animals touched and smelled one another with their trunks. Then Mbili backed off, turned, and ran a few paces. He came after her. Mbili stopped. The bull came up behind and rested his trunk and tusks on her back as he mounted her. After mating he stayed near Mbili and later they mated again. Although friendly, the bull was only interested in Mbili while she was ready to mate, and after a day he wandered off.

FAMILY LIFE

Mbili returned to her nursemaid duties. Whenever it rained heavily her new niece sheltered beneath her. There was plenty of food again and Mbili's sister easily made enough milk for the baby. The baby usually kept up with the herd as it moved, but if she lagged behind, her mother or Mbili would stay with her. Lions were charged on sight.

Throughout May and June the elephants had a quiet and easy time. As they slowly traveled across country they met other herds with new calves, but the young elephants were too small to meet and play and their mothers did not let them wander far from their side. Each herd had its own home area but these overlapped. During the course of the year the herds moved to different parts of the savanna, but at all times the older elephants knew where food, water, or danger might be found.

Now, toward the end of the second rainy season, the waterholes were full and the elephants enjoyed regular baths. Many other animals also used the waterholes but they usually moved out of the way when the elephants appeared. One evening a family of warthogs was drinking when the elephants arrived. The warthogs moved away but caught the attention of Mbili's young brother. He chased after one, and it trotted off rapidly with its tail in the air. The little elephant enjoyed this so much that he chased all the other warthogs one by one.

Playtime

The elephants made the most of the deep water. They disappeared beneath it leaving only their trunks visible, then rose up making huge waves. They squirted fountains of water in the air and at one another. They rolled and splashed about and even the oldest ones allowed the youngsters to climb all over them. The nine elephants seemed to be one big happy family.

▷ Young elephants are playful and engage in mock fights. They also are curious about objects they find, exploring them with their trunks.

Growing up

But Mbili's eleven-year-old cousin was becoming too rough. The cows had put up with his bumping and wrestling when he was small but now he was big and strong and was throwing his weight about too often. With tiny calves around the adults were anxious. One day he bumped into Mbili's mother, who hit him with a sideways swipe of her head. Then the big cows began to bang into him hard and often. He moved aside from the others. A few days later he joined up with a passing bull and left the herd.

Living in harmony with other animals

Mbili's life revolved around food and her family, but she was aware of other kinds of animal that lived beside her. Most of them she ignored. The herds of zebra, wildebeest, antelope, and giraffe had little effect on her life. For most of the year there was plenty of food for all, and at times of shortage she could reach food that other animals could not.

Perhaps the animals that affected Mbili most were the flies that buzzed around her face. Most other animals could be chased off, but even though she swung her tail and trunk and covered herself with mud, the flies still came. Egrets were also constant companions. Sometimes they walked alongside her. Sometimes they rode on her back. Mbili did not mind them.

As the dry season began, the earth once more became parched and dusty. But Mbili and her herd continued from season to season with their unhurried lives.

▷ Birds such as egrets often accompany elephants, feeding on insects stirred up as the elephant moves. They may also unwittingly act as sentries.

29

CONSERVATION

For thousands of years people have hunted elephants for food. While hunters had only bows and spears, hunting had little effect on elephant numbers. With firearms, many more elephants were killed, often just for trophies or ivory. Attempts have been made to stop the ivory trade but bans are hard to enforce and poaching and smuggling may still continue.

Elephants face another, more lasting danger. Human numbers are increasing. Farming needs to expand, taking over land that elephants once roamed. Their living space is gradually shrinking.

To conserve elephants, huge areas of land must be set aside so the animals can find food and live normal lives. In parts of Africa large nature reserves or national parks meet this need. But even within these areas there can be problems. Elephants learn which areas are safe and move in. Numbers may become greater than the land can support. Also, elephants break down trees and bushes. This can be useful as it opens up dense vegetation and helps provide food for other animals. If elephant numbers are small, new trees soon grow. But with too many elephants, the vegetation may have no chance to recover and the area can become useless to wildlife. Should some elephants be killed so that they do not all starve? Or should they be left in the hope that a balance will be reached? We are not sure of the answer, but the elephant's future may depend on it.

For further details
Useful information about elephant conservation can be obtained from the World Wildlife Fund,
1601 Connecticut Ave. N.W.
Washington, D.C. 20009.

Photo: Lee Lyon, Survival Anglia

▷ These young elephants are being moved from land needed for farming to a place where they can roam freely.